AF491018

Your notes and drawings ↑↑↑

Your notes and drawings ↑↑↑

Your notes and drawings ↑↑↑

Your notes and drawings ↑↑↑

Your notes and drawings ↑↑↑

Your notes and drawings ↑↑↑

Your notes and drawings ↑↑↑

Your notes and drawings ↑↑↑

Your notes and drawings ↑↑↑

Your notes and drawings ↑↑↑

Your notes and drawings ↑↑↑

Your notes and drawings ↑↑↑

Your notes and drawings ↑↑↑

Your notes and drawings ↑↑↑

Your notes and drawings ↑↑↑

Your notes and drawings ↑↑↑

Your notes and drawings ↑↑↑

Your notes and drawings ↑↑↑

Your notes and drawings ↑↑↑

Your notes and drawings ↑↑↑

Your notes and drawings ↑↑↑

Your notes and drawings ↑↑↑

Your notes and drawings ↑↑↑

Your notes and drawings ↑↑↑

Your notes and drawings ↑↑↑

Your notes and drawings ↑↑↑

Your notes and drawings ↑↑↑

Your notes and drawings ↑↑↑

Your notes and drawings ↑↑↑

Your notes and drawings ↑↑↑

Your notes and drawings ↑↑↑

Your notes and drawings ↑↑↑

Your notes and drawings ↑↑↑